THE STORY OF THE

PRIVY GARDEN

AT HAMPTON COURT

MAVIS BATEY

JAN WOUDSTRA

BARN ELMS

THE HISTORY OF THE PRIVY GARDEN

Mavis Batey
President of the Garden History Society

The royal Privy Garden at Hampton Court encapsulates the baroque spirit of the age of William and Mary. It is a rare example of formal 'stately' gardening in Britain, now accurately restored after scrupulous archaeological survey and detailed research in the archives. Once again, nearly 300 years after it was first conceived, King William's private garden forms a perfect complement to the majestic south façade of the palace as designed by Sir Christopher Wren.

Hampton Court has always been a show place. 'This is the most splendid and most magnificent royal palace of any that may be found in England or indeed in any other kingdom', a much-travelled sixteenth-century visitor wrote in his journal. However, Hampton Court was not always a royal palace. The building was begun by Thomas Wolsey in 1515, the year he received his cardinal's hat from Rome and was appointed Lord Chancellor by Henry VIII. Cardinal Wolsey, who was a great patron of the arts, employed Italian craftsmen in the building of his luxurious palace and entertained lavishly, with as many as 280 rooms kept ready to receive guests.

During the Tudor peace, when fortified castles were no longer needed, gardens and galleries could be constructed outside the walls of new palaces. Mediaeval castle gardens had been built in a haphazard fashion in leftover spaces between buildings and were 'pleasances' for the ladies. Renaissance gardens, in the words of the humanist Erasmus, were 'design'd for Pleasure; but for honest Pleasure, the Entertainment of the Sight, the Smell and the Refreshment of the very Mind'. In true Renaissance spirit, Wolsey's moated gardens to the north of the palace were chiefly for private meditation and he would, towards evening, intone divine service there with his chaplain in its 'arbours and alleys so pleasant and so dulce'.

Wolsey only enjoyed Hampton Court for ten years; by the summer of 1525 it had been conveyed with all its contents to Henry VIII. It was said that it was while the cardinal was strolling in his garden with the king

1 and 2. Portraits of William when Prince of Orange and Mary as Queen of England. William and Mary were offered the crown jointly after the exclusion of James II in 1688. William was the son of William of Orange and Charles II's sister, while Mary was the daughter of James II, Charles II's brother; they were therefore first cousins. Hampton Court became their favourite palace.

3. *Lion on the roof of the Great Hall. Such beasts stood on green and white posts in the Privy Garden. They were painted in bright colours and gilded, and held small vanes or flags emblazoned with arms and emblems.*

that the latter suddenly asked why he had felt moved to build so majestic a home. Wolsey, already sensing his impending fall from favour, replied: 'To show how noble a palace a subject may offer to his sovereign'. Henry VIII interpreted this 'offer' as a gift, but allowed Wolsey to remain as a tenant and to have the use of Richmond Palace for entertaining. After Wolsey's final fall from favour and death in 1529, Henry VIII remodelled Hampton Court, building a new Great Hall and a Water Gallery and elaborate royal gardens.

Henry VIII wanted his gardens not for solitary meditation but as an impressive heraldic accompaniment to his magnificent palace, which would outshine the chateaux of his rival Francis I in France. Important visitors would arrive by river at the Water Gallery, walk through covered galleries overlooking a chequerboard garden of squares of grass, white sand and brick dust, through a turreted pavilion, along another covered way to the south front entrance of the palace. Here, in the area in front of the royal apartments, was a garden full of Tudor emblems and imagery. Badges, banners and royal beasts, which had been erected in profusion on the pinnacles of the new palace roof, were similarly displayed on the ground, giving full value to the powerful regalia of a Tudor monarch.

The beasts, which included effigies of leopards, lions and unicorns, griffins and antelopes, were mounted on green and white poles, the Tudor colours. The craftsmen were kept busy changing the queen's beasts for each of Henry VIII's new wives; one payment in March 1537 is recorded for 'twenty vanes paynted and new alteryd from Queen Annes arms unto Queen Janes with theyr badges', and the true lovers' knots on the timbers were changed from AH to JH; this was for the ill-fated Jane Seymour, who would die at Hampton Court giving birth to the future Edward VI in the autumn after her emblems were erected.

The pond gardens to the west were also surrounded by striped poles supporting heraldic beasts, and although the ornamental fishponds have been filled in and made into flower gardens the low stone capped walls, with some of the bases on which the effigies stood, still remain. The most noticeable part of the king's Privy Garden was the triangular Mount Garden, which had a lantern arbour roofed with a lead cupola on the mount. This was approached by a cockleshell path bordered by yet more heraldic beasts. Nothing remains of this mount area (it was demolished by King William), but one of the bases of the Tudor towers, seen to the east of the heraldic garden, was discovered during the recent archaeology. The tower had served as a garden viewing pavilion on one side and a standing for observing the hunting in the park on the other.

4. *A detail of the* Panorama of Hampton Court from the Thames *drawn by Anthonis van Wyngaerde in about 1558. The drawing shows the heraldic garden, the onion-shaped dome of the Great Arbour in the Mount Garden and the Water Gallery in which Queen Mary resided while Wren was rebuilding the palace.*

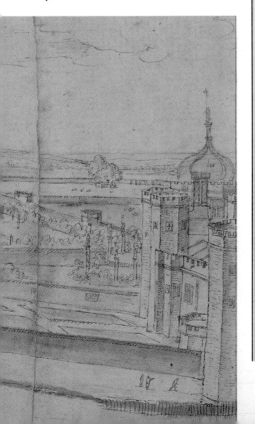

6. *William and Mary's hunting palace at Het Loo. The garden was painstakingly restored between 1977 and 1984. The seventeenth-century baroque garden had been overlaid by a garden in the fashionable English landscape style in 1806.*

5. *Part of the bird's-eye view of Hampton Court in 1702 by Leonard Knyff. The east parterre (known as the Great Fountain Garden) and patte d'oie of avenues leading into the park are in the foreground; the Privy Garden with the Tijou screens, Mary's bower and William's banqueting house are to the left of the palace.*

The Privy Garden was undoubtedly at its most splendid at the time of the Knyff painting of 1702, the year of William III's death, and it is to this period that the garden has now been restored. Meanwhile there had been several changes since Henry's heraldic gardens with their Tudor emblems. Travellers at the end of the sixteenth century commented on the whimsical artfully cut topiary shapes, 'men and women, half men and half horse, sirens, serving maids with baskets, French lilies and delicate crenellations,…all true to life and so cleverly and amusingly interwoven'. Queen Elizabeth, who frequently stayed at Hampton Court, had flower gardens made outside her apartments; a leaded bay window bearing the date mark 1568 can be seen overlooking the present knot garden, by the lower orangery in the pondyard area.

The Stuarts mainly used Hampton Court for hunting. Whitehall remained the official palace for the court, but Charles II hankered after a new palace at Greenwich. When in the country he preferred Windsor, as Hampton Court, where Oliver Cromwell used to spend his weekends, had unpleasant memories for him. Charles II introduced grand formal avenue planting into the hunting park, which John Evelyn had said had hitherto been 'a flat naked piece of ground', but the restricted Privy Garden layout had been simplified to grass quarters and fountains, which Pepys, in the pre-William era, had noted was 'our present fashion of gardens to make them plain'.

William III suffered from asthma and was determined to live upwind from London's polluted atmosphere. He used Whitehall as little as possible and gave Greenwich over for a naval hospital. Kensington Palace was built as a domestic residence, but, even before his coronation, Hampton Court was chosen as his new great palace. William and Mary paid their first visit to Hampton Court within a fortnight of Mary's arrival in England in February 1689 and fell in love with its rural riverside setting. Wren was immediately called in to modernise Henry's rambling old palace and so anxious were the royal couple to escape from London that, in spite of the building work, they spent much of their first summer at Hampton Court, superintending the new gardens, which were as important to them as the palace itself.

William and Mary had been devoted gardeners at their hunting palace of Het Loo, which was begun in 1684. Like all the other royal gardens in the Netherlands, the gardens had been supervised by William's great friend, Hans Willem Bentinck. Daniel Marot, the Hugenot refugee, who became William's decorative designer, was involved with the gardens as well as the interior of the palace. William and Mary resumed their gardening activities at Hampton Court always working as a team; Daniel Defoe put it nicely: 'the amendments and alterations were made by the King, or the Queen's particular special command, or by both; for their majesties agreed so well in their fancy, and had both so good judgement in the just proportions of things, which are the principal beauties of a garden, that it may be said they both ordered everything that was done'. Bentinck accompanied them to England to be created Earl of Portland and Superintendent of the Royal Gardens. Marot followed later.

Mary, who had been brought up in Charles II's court, dreaded the thought of a return to formality and intrigues. Hampton Court became for her the retreat where she could pursue the domestic life she loved: sewing, gardening and enjoying her prized collection of pictures and ceramics. Queen Mary's special delight was Henry VIII's Water Gallery with its balcony over the Thames. She had it refitted as private apartments, exquisitely furnished, for the use of herself and her ladies. A grotto was made in the stairwell. Defoe said, 'she ordered all the little, neat, curious Things to be done, which suited her own Convenience, and made it the pleasantest little Place within Doors, that could possibly be made'.

The special Delftware closet in the Water Gallery contained, according to Defoe, 'a vast stock of fine china ware, the like whereof was not then to be seen in England'. Fresh flowers were arranged, like Dutch still-life paintings, in blue and white vases, which stood on brackets and overmantels carved by Grinling Gibbons. Mary's combined interests in ceramics and flowers resulted in the making of Delftware flower pyramids, some of which can be seen in the palace. Each tier of the pyramid had cavities filled with damp moss for cut flowers, not exclusively for tulips, as is sometimes suggested. The patterns for the vases, as for the tiles in the Queen's Dairy, were by Daniel Marot, whose garden parterre designs echoed the decorative designs in his Delftware, floral marquetry and textiles.

Daniel Marot contributed to the new concept of the Franco-Dutch garden. The great French gardens, like Louis XIV's Versailles laid out by Le Nôtre, were spatially designed on central axes extending beyond boundary limits; artful contrivance of perspective was needed in the Dutch landscape with its grid-like patterns of drainage canals, and so garden-making became more intimate and inward looking. The Franco-Dutch compromise, therefore, allowed more attention to decorative detail and to horticulture in which the Dutch excelled. William III was praised

8. Mixed flowers typical of the time and including heartsease, day lily, peony, poppy, rose, martagon lily, French marigold, blackberry and hollyhock. Jakob van Walscapelle's painting is in the National Gallery.

7. A Delftware pagoda vase in the King's Apartments. Such vases, filled with cut flowers, were an original idea for Queen Mary, brilliantly reflecting her combined interests in ceramics and flowers.

Platte Bonde decoup de fleeurs.

5 Penssee diferentes.

D. Marot fec:

avec Priuileg:

9. *An illustration from Marot's* Nouveau Livre de Parterres, *1703. This shows various types of parterre for gardens clearly designed to be looked at from above, whether from windows or terraces. The* parterre à l'angloise, *which was the type used in the Privy Garden, is shown at the bottom*

*10. Engraving of the Privy Garden by
Sutton Nicholls of about 1696. It shows
the earlier gazon coupé or cutwork
design when the shapes were cut in
the turf. The Arethusa fountain in the
foreground was dismantled in the
second phase of the laying out of the
garden and is now in Bushy Park,
where it is known as the Diana
fountain.*

by Defoe for having revived 'the love of gardening'; inspired by
Kensington and Hampton Court, 'gentlemen followed every where, with
such a gust that the alteration is indeed wonderful throughout the whole
kingdom'.

Hampton Court had already seen French ideas brought back by
Charles II from exile, when André Mollet introduced the Grand Manner
into the park at the Restoration. William III retained his Long Water canal
and the semicircular arcade of limes and, under Wren, extended the *patte
d'oie*, or goosefoot of avenues, into the park. Not satisfied with grand
spatial concepts alone, however, the king employed Daniel Marot to
design *broderie* parterres to fill in the vast semicircle in the Great
Fountain Garden, as seen in the Knyff painting on page 6.

Such sophisticated parterres, derived from earlier knot gardens, were
new to England and the French term denotes their origin. André Mollet,
who published *Le Jardin de Plaisir* in 1651 showing intricate *broderie*
designs, had already created a parterre for Charles I at St James's Palace.
Daniel Marot published his *Nouveau Livre de Parterres* in 1703 and this
included various types of parterre which are relevant to Hampton Court.

The first illustration is of a *parterre de pièces coupées pour les fleurs*,
where the shapes, containing special plants, form an overall flowing
scroll design, edged with box and with gravel paths all round; below are
parterres de broderie, embroidery-like flowery designs made of dwarf box
against a background of coloured earth; the sparsely planted flowers and

clipped evergreens were grown separately in *plates-bandes* – the long thin mounded borders that edged the shapes. In *parterres à l'angloise* the internal shapes are patterned in grass and outlined with *plates-bandes*. At Hampton Court the parterres in the centre of the Great Fountain Garden were of *broderie* and those in the Privy Garden *à l'angloise*, to display the excellence of English turf.

The Privy Garden had at first a simple *gazon coupé* English parterre. This means it was basically grass with shapes cut out of the turf and filled with coloured gravels, as seen on the engraving by Sutton Nicholls. King Henry's mount had been partially demolished and terraces raised to east and west for viewing platforms. It was also intended that the Water Gallery, where Queen Mary was temporarily housed, would be removed when Wren's palace was finished, so that the Privy Garden could be extended and replanned. It had already been widened to match the new south façade of the enlarged palace, where the King's Apartments were being built.

Although the parterre garden was at this stage flowerless, the pondyard area to the west of the Water Gallery was converted into a botanical garden for the flower-loving queen. Above it was Queen Mary's Bower, a long tunnel arbour or shelter planted with wych elm over a wooden frame in 1690. Mary liked to go there and sew and do 'knotting' with her ladies. Queen Mary encouraged the collecting of rare plants, taking advantage of the opportunities for obtaining plants through Dutch trade with the East Indies and of learning from the Dutch experts about their cultivation. Not content with her East Indian and Cape of Good Hope collections, the queen sent plant collectors to Virginia and the Canary Islands.

In order to house her 'exotics' or plants from overseas the queen had 'glass cases' or 'stoves' built in the area of the old pondyard and her collections, many of which were brought from the Netherlands, were placed in the care of her personal botanist, Dr Leonard Plukenet. The queen's exotics and 'stoves' attracted the attention of other gardening virtuosi or 'curious persons', such as the Duchess of Beaufort and Charles Hatton, a noted botanical collector, who saw 'about 400 rare Indian plantes, which were never seen in England' when he visited Hampton Court in 1690. He also saw 'the finest collection of amaranths and hollyoke I believe were ever seen'.

Two of the three drained ponds in the old pondyard, which became known as the Glass Case Garden, were planted with florists' flowers as these greatly interested the queen. One was entirely devoted to auriculas.

11. *Limewood carving by Grinling Gibbons. Gibbons's exquisite carvings of flowers, fruit and foliage can be seen on the overmantels surrounding several of the portraits in the King's Apartments at Hampton Court.*

12. *Illustration from the 'Codex Honselaerdicensis'. This manuscript is a series of drawings of a plant collection acquired by William III in the Netherlands and transported to Hampton Court in 1692. The collection included rare exotics which would have been grown in sophisticated 'stoves', and also several varieties of bulbs. This page shows a tulip reminiscent of Duc van Tol 'Aurora' (see photograph on page 32), auriculas and various anemones.*

The term florists' flowers applied to a small group of plants cultivated to perfection, as was the tulip during the Dutch tulipomania of the 1630s.

Queen Mary had pitifully little time in which to enjoy her garden and collections as she died of smallpox in December 1694, only five years after she had set up house in her beloved Water Gallery, where she could retreat to 'a sweet and quiet life'. She never used the splendid palace apartments designed for her by Wren and after her death her husband lost interest in Hampton Court and the gardens she had so loved.

Virtually no work was done there until 1699, when in April William paid his first visit for five years. Before he left for the Netherlands he ordered that the palace should be made ready to receive the court as Whitehall Palace had been put out of action by a disastrous fire. The Broad Walk and the Pavilion Terrace stretching along the Thames to a new bowling green were planned for his courtiers to stroll along, and on his return the king's attention turned once again to his own Privy Garden.

The king now needed expanded private gardens, not only owing to increased activity at the palace, but because the Treaty of Rijswijk in 1697 brought a respite from European wars. Hitherto he had been forced to spend all his summers campaigning and only saw his gardens in the winter, when he consoled himself with his evergreens, which he said were 'the greatest addition to the beauty of a garden, preserving the figure of a place, even in the roughest part of an inclement and tempestuous winter'.

The lower part of Wren's building leading on to the terrace above the Privy Garden had been made into an orangery and put in the charge of a Dutch gardener, Hendrik Quellenburg, who was responsible for the king's tender greens, the Dutch bays, phillyrea, myrtles, oleander, alaternus and the orange trees, so prized as a symbol of the House of Orange. The Water Gallery was demolished in 1700 by royal command from the Netherlands and its Grinling Gibbons carvings, made to offset the queen's Delftware, were later set up in a new castellated banqueting house built out of an old Tudor garden tower by the river.

A new player comes on the scene for this second phase of the layout of the Privy Garden, 'the most Industrious and knowing Mr Wise', as Evelyn called him. Henry Wise, whose name first appears in the Hampton Court accounts in 1699, was a partner with George London in the famous Brompton Park nursery, founded in 1681. Their trade expanded considerably in the reign of William and Mary and they supplied most of the great gardens with seeds, bulbs, shrubs and trees, specialising in shaped evergreens and the 'moveable' plants, or plants in pots, which the

13. *Portrait of Henry Wise (1653-1738). Wise, who was largely responsible for laying out the Privy Garden as now restored, was George London's partner in a famous nursery and landscaping practice. His name first appears at Hampton Court in 1699. This portrait from the Royal Collection is by Godfrey Kneller.*

15 far right. *The gardener and his wheelbarrow in this detail from Decker's painting of the Provenier's house in Haarlem is an archetypal image from a Dutch garden of the early eighteenth century.*

14. *Illustration of garden tools from John Evelyn's 'Elysium Britannicum' of about 1659. Tools like these would have been used in the Privy Garden. Number 31 is 'a roller for gravell walkes, the best are made of the hardest marble, and such as are procured from the ruines of many places in Smyrna when old columns of demolished Antiquities being saw'd off, towards the vino of the pedistall and at the part or modell where the shaft deminishes makes excellent rollers'. Those in the Privy Garden were made of Portland stone.*

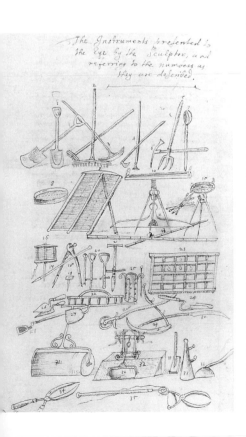

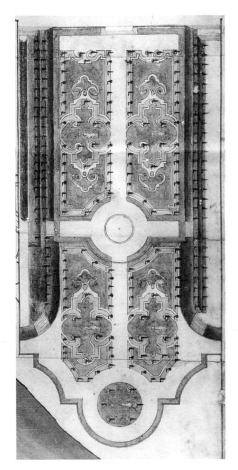

17. *Part of an early eighteenth-century plan of Hampton Court which includes the Privy Garden. This plan is held in the Soane Museum and has been used as the basis of the reconstruction.*

16. *A detail of the Privy Garden from the Knyff painting shown on page 6. The recent archaeology has proved just how accurate the painting is, even in the smallest detail.*

king had made so popular. They also provided formal garden designs, based on French techniques, which they codified in *The Retir'd Gard'ner*, published in 1706.

Although Henry Wise had contracted for and was responsible for the laying out of the *parterre à l'angloise*, the design may still owe something to Daniel Marot, who had returned to the Netherlands in 1698 before the second phase of the making of the Privy Garden began. George London, who was Deputy Superintendent of the Royal Gardens, would also have been involved in the planning. Christopher Wren, both architect and mathematician, had always taken the 'great lines' and perspective of Hampton Court's layout as part of his overall remit as Surveyor of Works, believing that the true test for the 'causes of beauty' was 'natural or geometrical beauty'.

The laying out of the Privy Garden had been by no means straight-forward for all those concerned owing to the king's indecision about his requirements once the garden was doubled in size and the Water Gallery removed. A major factor in the new design was that William wanted to see the barges on the Thames from the Orangery. The garden was lowered eight feet and Queen Henrietta Maria's great Arethusa fountain by Le Sueur, which Cromwell had had removed to the Privy Garden from Somerset House, was dismantled. London and Wise had already planted the magnificent Chestnut Avenue in Bushy Park as the intended grand new approach to the palace.

Henry Wise had laid down a first parterre in the Privy Garden when, in the spring of 1701, he and William Talman, the architect, were required to prepare new designs and a wooden model of the garden to show the king. The beautiful grey wrought-iron screens, made by Jean Tijou, and originally intended for the Great Fountain Garden, were put up at the end of the Privy Garden to see the effect. The king decided the ground would have to be lowered even further to achieve a view of the river through the screens and so Wise's first parterre had to be scrapped. Wise immediately undertook to reduce the levels further and to lay out the new parterres. The work proceeded with such speed that the parterre was almost complete when William III died unexpectedly in 1702.

The Privy Garden was modified by Queen Anne, who removed all the parterre edgings because, according to Defoe, she disliked the smell of box, and in any case, having always detested her brother-in-law, she would have been anxious to change his garden. She only made occasional use of Hampton Court, where, in Alexander Pope's famous lines, she would 'sometimes counsel take – and sometimes tea'.

The formal shape of the Privy Garden and the clipped evergreens were retained, however, even after Addison and Pope had campaigned against mathematical topiary as 'deviations from nature'. Hampton Court was singled out by eighteenth-century improvers as the bastion of regularity, and foreign visitors were amazed to find nothing to show of the much vaunted English landscape style in a royal palace. 'Capability' Brown, when he became royal gardener and moved to Wilderness House in the gardens in 1764, was asked by George III to undertake landscape improvements, but declined to do so, it is said, 'out of respect to himself and his profession'. He was probably influenced by his friend, across Bushy Park, Horace Walpole, who, as an antiquarian, would have favoured historic associations in spite of his advocacy of landscape gardening.

George III never lived at Hampton Court, preferring Richmond and Windsor, and Brown continued to maintain the royal garden as he found it. He planted the Great Vine in 1768. Brown could not, however, bring himself to clip the yews and hollies formally and Thomas Jefferson on a visit to England just after Brown's death noted that they were running completely wild. George IV thought so little of the Privy Garden that he removed its statuary to Windsor, leaving only the plinths and sundials.

It was the historian Ernest Law who made a study of Hampton Court's garden history in 1890. He revived old names – the Pond Garden, the Tiltyard and the Wilderness – and laid out the Tudor knot garden and the new Pond Garden by William III's banqueting house. His revival schemes included clipping the original yews in the Great Fountain Garden into the giant cones we see today. Law's greatest contribution was the reinstatement of the Tijou screens, which had been dispersed to several museums throughout the country, at the end of the Privy Garden. Queen Victoria had opened the palace to the public in 1838 and the Privy Garden was planted with shrubs and flower-bordered walks, which were at first kept private for 'Grace and Favour' residents. Generations of their children used to love playing peek-a-boo with their nannies in the overgrown shrubberies.

By this time these picturesque thickets had totally obliterated both the original fleur de lis decorative design of the parterre viewed from King William's first floor state apartments and the grand baroque concept of the relationship of Wren's architecture and the geometry of the garden as seen through the Tijou screens from the river. The tercentenary of the Glorious Revolution in 1988 was highlighted by exhibitions and publications bringing together the architecture and gardening of William

18 and 19. Photographs of Queen Mary's Bower and the central walk in the Privy Garden taken in the 1920s. Nannies and their charges have taken the place of king and queen, but the knuckled wych elms were a tribute to generation after generation of palace gardener. Sadly the elms succumbed to Dutch elm disease in the 1970s.

20. Drawing by Leonard Knyff of the Privy Garden from the south, 1702.

21. Photograph taken from a crane in 1994 during the archaeological investigations. The viewpoint matches that of the Knyff drawing of 1702 shown above.

22. Before serious archaeology could begin all vegetation had to be removed from the Privy Garden. A crane lifting one of the mature trees that was replanted in the Home Park.

and Mary's reign both here and in the Netherlands. Attention was drawn to the restoration of Het Loo, which, in 1806, had been overlaid with a *jardin anglais* by Louis Napoleon, but had recently been restored to its formal William and Mary glories.

The Garden History Society mounted a tercentenary exhibition in the King's Apartments, showing on pedestals in the windows what the gardens outside would have looked like in William's time. The disastrous fire had taken place two years before and much restoration was being done in the palace. The Privy Garden was sealed off while the scaffolding was up along the terrace and it might have been the time to have looked historically at the garden, as at Het Loo, but, although there had been a Royal Parks historical survey back in 1982, the climate in England was not yet favourable for authentic garden restoration.

However, when, in 1990, Historic Royal Palaces was set up as an agency, a commendable initiative was taken to treat the palace and its gardens as an entity, as Wren and William and Mary had planned. In 1992, in the process of extensive public consultation, options for the restoration of the Privy Garden were exhibited and included a model, reminiscent of Wise's laborious undertaking for King William. Archaeological investigation followed the next year.

The results of the excavation exceeded all expectations when the fleur de lis pattern of Wise's parterre, corresponding perfectly with contemporary plans, began to appear in the three foot deep soil-enriched planting trenches of the *plates-bandes*, which formed the basis of the design for each of the quarter plots. The Thames gravel in which the *plates-bandes* were embedded must have prevented destruction by tunnelling moles. The creatures are established in the park where, after all, William's horse had stumbled on a molehill with fatal consequence.

Once the archaeology had been recorded and transferred to accurate drawings, turf was laid down in 1995 and the patterns pegged out to be recut and planted. Even the drainage system had been discovered intact and the plinths unearthed during the excavation were made ready to receive the statuary. Some of the holes in which William's beloved pyramid yews had been planted to give 'figure' to the Privy Garden were also discovered along the flanking terraces.

At a time when historic parks and gardens are arousing such interest it is important that one of the greatest of our royal palaces now has a rare example of a magnificent formal garden. The authenticity of the restoration of the Privy Garden is a great tribute to all those who have contributed to this splendid rediscovery.

THE RECONSTRUCTION OF THE PRIVY GARDEN

Jan Woudstra

Environmental Design Associates

The reconstruction of the Privy Garden began in earnest after the exhibition at Hampton Court in 1992 in which various possibilities for restoration were put forward. One proposal was for wholesale restoration, while another suggested partial restoration allowing the historic trees to remain. The latter presented several problems, not the least of which was that if the trees were left at their then size it would not be possible to reopen a clear view to the Thames. The trees could not be reduced to their original size since none of them would be likely to rejuvenate if cut down so drastically. In the end the response for a wholesale restoration was overwhelming and was supported by the Royal Household, English Heritage and the Garden History Society.

Following this positive response the decision was taken to go ahead with a complete restoration and an ambitious schedule was drawn up to allow the garden to be reopened in 1995. The works included propagation from the original holly and yew trees so that the garden could be replanted from the same stock; searching for an appropriate box edging; setting up a trial area; removing all the vegetation from the Privy Garden in the late winter of 1993, and taking a number of trees which were of horticultural importance to the nursery in Home Park, where they were planted in a special area as a collection of specimens. The most extensive garden archaeology ever undertaken to allow restoration work to take place was completed in August 1994. Meanwhile landscape historians and architects had been drawing up plans for the reinstatement of the garden to be ready in time for a royal opening scheduled for 6 July 1995.

The archaeology uncovered the outlines of the garden much as it was laid out in 1701-2. The garden was designed on a south-facing rectangular plot of about 230 by 90 yards. It was divided in four quarters with a fountain in the centre and terraces running along both the east and west sides. Each of the quarters was surrounded by *plates-bandes* (the decorative bands described on page 12), and there were central

23. Winter 1993. The felled yews lying in front of the Tijou screen. Ring counts confirmed that several were planted almost 300 years ago and vertical sections showed that they were kept at eight foot high for about 35 years. Before the trees were felled cuttings were taken and the young trees are now being grown on and will eventually replace those planted for the opening.

23

plates-bandes within each of these quarters. Study of the archaeological findings showed that the parterre had been laid out on a four foot grid which determined the layout of the walks and *plates-bandes*. This basic grid is also the reason why imperial measurements have been used throughout the reconstruction exercise.

The research into the planting revealed five late seventeenth-century plant lists (now in the British Museum) relating to Queen Mary's collections, an herbarium (in the Natural History Museum) and there was also a full set of accounts in the Public Record Office which included two 1701 lists of plants ordered for the Privy Garden. These were helpful in determining some of the more important elements in the garden, but there was no surviving complete list. The records revealed that round headed variegated hollies and pyramid yews were not the only clipped trees, but that there were also four *Phillyrea latifolia* L. and four *Rhamnus alaternus* L., both popular seventeenth and early eighteenth-century plants, which would have been planted in key positions within the design. There were also large numbers of shrubs, such as sweet briars (*Rosa rubiginosa* L.), syringas (*Philadelphus coronarius* L.), standard honeysuckles (*Lonicera*), lavender (*Lavandula angustifolia* Miller), savin (*Juniperus sabina* L.) and variegated rhus (*Coriaria myrtifolia* L. 'Variegata'). The lists of plants ordered also included tulips, white daffodils, crocus, hyacinth and bulbous iris. The bulbous plants all related to the spring planting, and there were no records of perennials and annuals which might also have been used, but which would have been grown in the garden's own nurseries and so would in any case have been less likely to appear on lists. It also emerged that one of the lists of plants ordered referred to the planting of the lower half of the garden only, and that these records, too, were therefore incomplete. There remained several questions to be answered: what other plants might have been used in the garden; where might the plants be acquired, and how would they have been arranged within the garden?

To answer these questions it was obviously essential to investigate contemporary planting practice. The research into this suggested that the manner of planting related to that practised at Longleat and Chatsworth, but differed from contemporary Dutch practice, or that practised by 'florists', the collectors of individual flowers. The positioning of the yew pyramids and round headed hollies was a relatively easy matter to establish, since there were the surviving trees and topographical evidence in the parterre area, and clear archaeological evidence on the terraces. The clipped trees down the

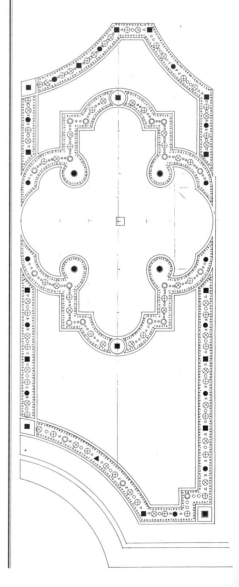

24. Reconstruction of the summer planting in the plates-bandes *of one half of the lower parterre.*

26. Spring bulbs from the 'Codex Honselaerdicensis' (see page 13). Shown here are a tulip, a white narcissus, blue hyacinths and some anemones.

25. Enlargement of part of 24 with key to the planting.
a. Pot marigold, b. Snapdragon,
c. French marigold, d. Red valerian,
e. Love-in-a-mist, f. Flower gentle,
p. Dwarf convolvulus, q. African marigold, r. Cornflower, s. Feverfew,
t. Yellow lupin, u. Eryngium planum.

Reading from top right the shrubs down the centre are as follows; Pyramid yew, Round headed variegated holly, Provence rose, Sweet briar, Philadelphus, Lavender, Savin, Variegated rhus, Dutch honeysuckle.

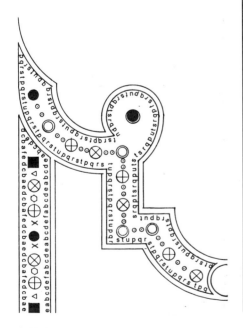

28 and 29. *A Dutch engraving showing an orange tree being moved in the seventeenth century and a photograph of the same operation taken at Hampton Court in 1995.*

27. *An orange tree from the ceiling of the King's Little Bedchamber which Antonio Verrio painted in 1701. He also decorated the banqueting house and one of its festoons appears on the title page. From 1685 Verrio held the title of Royal Gardener at St James's.*

centre line of the *plates-bandes* were interspersed with tall and low shrubs arranged in a regular rhythm. The positioning of the bulbs and summer planting was the most difficult part to resolve; English practice suggested that the plants would have been arranged in rows with the tallest plants in the centre row and the shorter plants in the side rows. The centre rows at the Privy Garden would have been taken up by the clipped trees and shrubs, so there would only have been space for a single row of flowers on either side of the *plates-bandes*. These flowers would likewise have been arranged in a rhythmic pattern of repeated plants. Although these borders contained all the components of a twentieth-century border, the way in which they were arranged was very different since they were not planted in large groups according to colour, but as a 'mixture enamel'd with all sorts of colours'.

The practice of renewing the planting for the different seasons was also tackled differently in each country. In France three seasonal changes were the normal practice, but there were times at the Trianon in Versailles when plants were changed every fortnight by using flowers in pots. There is no record of so many changes in England; two annual changes appear to have been the norm, one in July, when annuals were planted in the beds, and one in the autumn for spring planting. Individual plants may also have been replaced once they finished flowering. These changes in the *plates-bandes* were not the only seasonal change. During the summer exotic plants in pots would be carried outside and placed in prominent positions. Orange trees were placed in corner positions, where squares had been specially laid out for the purpose. These trees were overwintered in the orangery and moved outside in the summer. During the winter large pyramid yews were planted in the squares, only to be moved again before the summer. Such treatment could not have done the yews much good.

The *plates-bandes* were bordered by box edging, which made a permanent evergreen boundary and prevented the mixing of sand, soil and gravel. Box edging required the use of a specially selected dwarf strain of box, *Buxus sempervirens* L. 'Suffruticosa', which was first used in the Netherlands towards the end of the Middle Ages, but soon became popular all over Europe. This box is particularly suitable for keeping only a few inches high and wide, and would have been maintained by one or two annual clippings.

The *plates-bandes* were separated from the central grass areas by bands of sand a foot wide (known at the time as alleys). This was a local sand dug out of a pit in the park and it served to give a visual contrast.

On the other side only the box hedging separated the *plates-bandes* from the gravel walks. The gravel for these was excavated in the Privy Garden itself. Wire hurdles (see number 9 in John Evelyn's illustration on page 15) were used to separate the coarser gravel from the finer. The fine gravel was used for the top layer, while the coarser material was used as the foundation. The gravel walks at Hampton Court were given frequent rollings with three and a half foot wide Portland stone rollers.

The largest area of the parterre was covered by grass. Grass had been a main element in English parterres since the early seventeenth century, and English grass husbandry was famous abroad. William III even exported an English gardener, who rejoiced in the name of Mr Moss, to maintain his lawns at Het Loo. The grass would have arrived in turfs measuring one foot by three from nearby Molesey Hurst, where the finest grass, grazed by sheep, had been selected. During the growing season it would have been mown very short twice weekly with a scythe and rolled daily with a green wooden roller to remove any wormcasts and keep the surface even.

The *plates-bandes* were filled with good garden soil enriched with waste from latrines and the beds were rounded up along the centre to set off the plants and keep their roots dry. Contemporary texts refer to these mounded beds as 'ass's back' or 'carp's back'.

It is not surprising that most of the original sources would not be able to supply the plant material that was now required. Turf had to be specially grown by a specialist firm in Romney Marsh working to a specification based on the type of grass found in lowland heaths that would have grown at Molesey Hurst.

The perennials and annuals in the eighteenth century would have been grown by the gardens themselves from seed, but for the reopening a north Hampshire nursery specialising in historic plants was asked to provide 6200 plants of the sixteen different species required for the first seasonal planting scheme. The outer *plates-bandes* of the upper parterre are planted with nearly 400 of each of the following: Pot marigold (*Calendula officinalis* L.), larkspur (*Consolida ambigua* (L.) Ball & Heyw.), African marigold (*Tagetes erecta* L.), sweet scabious (*Sixalix atropurpurea* (L.) Greuter & Burdet 'Prolifera'), tall blue lobelia (*Lobelia syphilitica* L.) and nearly 200 sneezewort (*Achillea ptarmica* L. 'Flore Pleno'). The outer *plates-bandes* of the lower parterre are planted with coming on for 300 of each of the following: Pot marigold (*Calendula officinalis* L.), snapdragon (*Antirrhinum majus* L.), French marigold (*Tagetes patula* L.), red valerian (*Centranthus ruber* (L.) DC.),

31. *Summer Flowers by Rachel Ruysch (1664-1750). This beautiful painting in the National Gallery shows a number of favourite garden flowers, including columbine, auricula, honeysuckle, gardener's garters, snowball, day lily, peonies, hawthorn and French marigold. In* The Retir'd Gard'ner *London and Wise wrote of the marigold, 'Tho' the Marigold has no very agreeable Smell, yet it looks well in a Garden, its Flowers growing in Rays, and being of a beautiful Yellow'.*

30. *Engraving of gardeners and courtiers on the bowling green at Het Loo. No doubt Mr Moss himself is at work with the scythe.*

32. The variegated hollies and pyramid yews in the nursery at Hampton Court. The trees were imported from Italy and the Netherlands but acclimatised in England for a year before being planted in the Privy Garden. Young cone shaped yews are always described as pyramids, just as they were in the seventeenth century.

33. Thirty thousand box plants stood under the warm walls of the Hampton Court nursery before being planted out in the spring of 1995.

34. *The trial ground where varieties of box from the Netherlands, France and England were tested. They were all of the same shrubby variety of* **Buxus sempervirens** *'Suffructicosa', but the variation in habit, leaf size and colour was striking. After much deliberation an English strain was selected.*

love-in-a-mist (*Nigella damascena* L.) and about 250 flower gentle (*Amaranthus tricolor* L.). The central *plates-bandes* in both the upper and lower parterres are planted with the best part of 500 of each of the following: Dwarf convolvulus (*Convolvulus tricolor* L.), African marigold (*Tagetes erecta* L.), cornflower (*Centaurea cyanus* L.), feverfew (*Tanacetum parthenium* (L.) Schultz-Bip.), yellow lupin (*Lupinus luteus* L.) and about 250 *Eryngium planum* L. In all the borders the plants are repeated in a rhythmical pattern and are spaced one foot apart. There are almost 2000 marigolds in the Privy Garden.

The original box for the gardens had been imported from the Netherlands, but the 2500 yards required for the reinstatement of the garden was cultivated by a specialist boxwood nursery in Hampshire. They took 30,000 cuttings in late 1993 and each was planted in a separate plastic pot after the roots had formed.

The original yews and hollies are being propagated so that they can eventually be replanted in the Privy Garden, but it will be several years before they are a good size. Meanwhile as a stop gap, fully grown yews (*Taxus baccata* L.) have been brought over from the Netherlands and hollies (*Ilex aquifolium* L. 'Argentea Marginata') from Italy. These, and all the required shrubs, were imported and grown on for a year so that they could be fully acclimatised. One shrub, *Coriaria myrtifolia* L.'Variegata', could not be located anywhere in Europe. The eighteenth-century pyramids were kept at a height of about eight foot, the round headed hollies at a height of about four and a half to five foot, and the taller shrubs (the roses and philadelphus) would have been kept clipped into a ball shape about three and a half foot high. The shorter shrubs, such as lavender, savin and coriaria would have been about one to one and a half foot high.

The situation with contemporary bulbs is even trickier as very few historic varieties survive even in specialist collections. With the help of the famous historic bulb collection at Hortus Bulborum in Limmen in the Netherlands, a limited number of historic varieties has been acquired. In the coming years attempts will be made to make the planting more and more authentic as historic varieties are recovered and propagated in sufficient numbers for the Privy Garden. The favourite bulbs in the seventeenth century were tulips, especially those with variegated petals. These markings were most often caused by viruses which eventually killed the bulbs. This is one reason why none of the much depicted tulips in contemporary paintings survive, except for 'Zomerschoon' ('Summer Beauty'), a variety of which only a few hundred bulbs survive and which

is slow to propagate. The other reason why these bulbs do not exist any more is that nurserymen do not like virus diseased bulbs as the infection is spread by greenfly. It will therefore be difficult to obtain sufficient variegated tulips for the Privy Garden. There are a very few other early tulips, notably the Duc van Tol hybrids, which produce variegation without viruses and still survive. These are small tulips; Tulipa 'Aurora' is one such, with bright red and yellow variegated flowers. But even of this there are nowhere near enough to fill the whole of the Privy Garden. The paintings at Hampton Court by Verrio mainly show the larger varieties which may now be lost forever. But there is now a chance that nurserymen may be able to produce identical-looking flowers which could be used instead.

The evidence for most of the hard elements was much more clear-cut. Although some of the statuary had been moved away, it was known where all the items were. Sadly most of the original sculptures were too friable to be stood outside. These have now been resculpted in a London studio from Carrara marble. Two of the lead statues, originally painted a stone colour and placed on top of the south façade of the palace (see the Knyff painting on page 6), are still in the gardens, now in front of the upper orangery. One of the marble sundials on either side of the top steps was found in Kew Gardens and has been returned to Hampton Court. The terraces, walls and fountain in the centre have all been subject to conservation work. The central stone terrace steps have been reconstructed on the original foundations which were exposed by the

*35 top left. **The Hortus Bulborum in Limmen in the Netherlands. This is a botanical garden devoted to bulbs and is funded and maintained by the Association of Dutch bulb growers as a gene pool.***

*36. **Duc van Tol 'Aurora'. One of the few contemporary tulips which produces stripes without a virus.***

37. Photograph taken in the studio when the statues for the Privy Garden were being resculpted.

38. *Spring 1995: A view from the King's Apartments as work progresses.*

39. *Bacchus, signifying abundance, reinstated on his pedestal in 1995. The statue of Apollo, symbolising William III as the sun, was placed on the central vista.*

archaeologists. The pair of southern steps were rebuilt in oak on the basis that there could not have been stone steps in these positions because the archaeologists found no foundations of any substance. All the same it was clear that there would have been steps here and so they must have been of a lighter construction. Since Willem Bentinck, William III's adviser on matters of design, had wooden steps up his terrace in his garden at Zorgvliet in the Netherlands, it is likely that a similar construction was used at Hampton Court. One of the most tedious restoration projects is the cleaning of the blackened Tijou screen. This will be painted in the original pale grey 'iron colour', but it is a slow process and will take a number of years to complete.

The one most spectacular element in the garden is without doubt the Queen's Bower. This has been reconstructed in line with the archaeological and archival evidence. The original wych elm trees which used to cover the bower survived until the 1970s when they succumbed to Dutch elm disease. Their subsequent removal damaged the potential archaeological findings, but just enough information could be recovered

40. *The newly rebuilt Queen Mary's Bower is once again the dramatic feature that it has always been.*

to establish the twelve-foot width of the bower and its original length of about 100 yards. The bower was part of the first phase of William and Mary's garden-making in 1690 and the position of the central opening did not quite relate to the centre line of William III's layout. The eighteen foot high reconstructed bower, built with 74 oak arches and fir rails, like its historic precedent, repeats this discrepancy. A portico has been built at the northern end of the bower. This was visible on several of the earlier illustrations and was included in the accounts. A reproduction has been built which is a modern interpretation of a drawing found in a book of contemporary designs for Hampton Court. Elm disease is still a lethal danger, so hornbeam has been used for the replanting. A total of 296 trees of between 6 and 8 foot high have been planted. It is thought that they will need five to ten years before they fully grow over the wooden arches and meet at the top. They will be trained to the bower with willow ties taken from willows along the Thames and given an annual clip.

It was not possible for all the features to be faithfully reconstructed and a number of concessions have had to be made to cope with today's

41. *May 1995: The turf is laid, the shapes are cut out, the* plates-bandes *are mounded up to a carp's back, box edging, yew pyramids and hollies are being planted just as they were in 1701–2.*

requirements on such matters as health and safety, fire access and maintenance. Although these have been fitted in as sympathetically as possible they will be spotted by sharp-eyed visitors. Some features cannot be perfect from the beginning and it will be several years before some of the plants have reached their optimum size and shape. There is also the matter of trying out the original methods of caring for such a garden and seeing how these affect the overall picture as it develops.

The final outcome of all that has been done is that King William's Privy Garden can now be visited and admired in a way that has never before been possible. In the early eighteenth century most visitors would have been restricted to the Fountain Garden. Long before the gardens were opened in the nineteenth century plant growth had significantly altered the character of the Privy Garden. Only now is the secret Williamite garden finally and triumphantly revealed to all.

Note to readers: For the fullest account of the historical and archaeological research into the Privy Garden see *The Privy Garden* (Apollo, 1995), edited by Dr Simon Thurley, with contributions from David Jacques, Brian Dix and Jan Woudstra.

The Garden History Society takes a leading role in promoting all aspects of garden history and conservation. New members are welcome. For details apply to the Membership Secretary, Mrs Anne Richards, 5 The Knoll, Hereford HR1 1RU.

Barn Elms Publishing, 93 Castelnau, London SW13 9EL
First published 1995. Reprinted 1996
Text © 1995 Mavis Batey and Jan Woudstra
All rights reserved
Printed and bound in Great Britain by The Bath Press Colourbooks, Glasgow
ISBN 1 899531 01 7

A Barn Elms Handbook

Photographic sources and acknowledgements.
Front cover: Jan Davidsz. de Heem, *Still life with flowers* (Private Collection, USA), Edward Speelman Ltd.
Historic Royal Palaces, Crown copyright: *Title page* (photo Earl Beesley); 3 (photo C. Birtchnell); 11 (photo Earl Beesley); 20 (photo © British Museum); 21 (photo R. Fielding); 22; 24 and 25 (photos Environmental Design Associates); 27 (photo Earl Beesley); 37.
1, 2: by courtesy of the National Portrait Gallery, London; 4: Ashmolean Museum, Oxford; 5, 7, 13, 16: The Royal Collection © Her Majesty the Queen; 6: John Rotheroe; 8, 31: Reproduced by courtesy of the Trustees, The National Gallery, London; 9, 25, 28, 30, 35, 36: Jan Woudstra; 10: Master and Fellows, Magdalene College, Cambridge; 12, 26: Giorgio Galetti (© Biblioteca Nazionale, Florence); 14: Mark Laird; 15: Frans Hals Museum, Haarlem; 17: by courtesy of the Trustees of Sir John Soane's Museum; 18, 19: National Monuments Record (© RCHME); 29: Royal Horticultural Society, Lindley Library; 32, 33, 34, 38, 39, 40, 41: Jessica Smith.